TRURO
IN
50
BUILDINGS

CHRISTINE PARNELL

AMBERLEY

Acknowledgements

My thanks to those who helped me in any way to complete this book. If I have overlooked anyone please accept my apologies. Graham Coad, John Lean, Kathryn Oatey, David Parnell, Kingsley Wright and Diana Smith.

For Daniel, Darcey, Timothy and Caitlin

First published 2018

Amberley Publishing, The Hill, Stroud
Gloucestershire GL5 4EP

www.amberley-books.com

Copyright © Christine Parnell, 2018

The right of Christine Parnell to be identified as the Author of this work has been asserted in accordance with the Copyrights, Designs and Patents Act 1988.

Map contains Ordnance Survey data © Crown copyright and database right [2018]

British Library Cataloguing in Publication Data.
A catalogue record for this book is available from the British Library.

ISBN 978 1 4456 7861 0 (print)
ISBN 978 1 4456 7862 7 (ebook)

Origination by Amberley Publishing.
Printed in Great Britain.

Contents

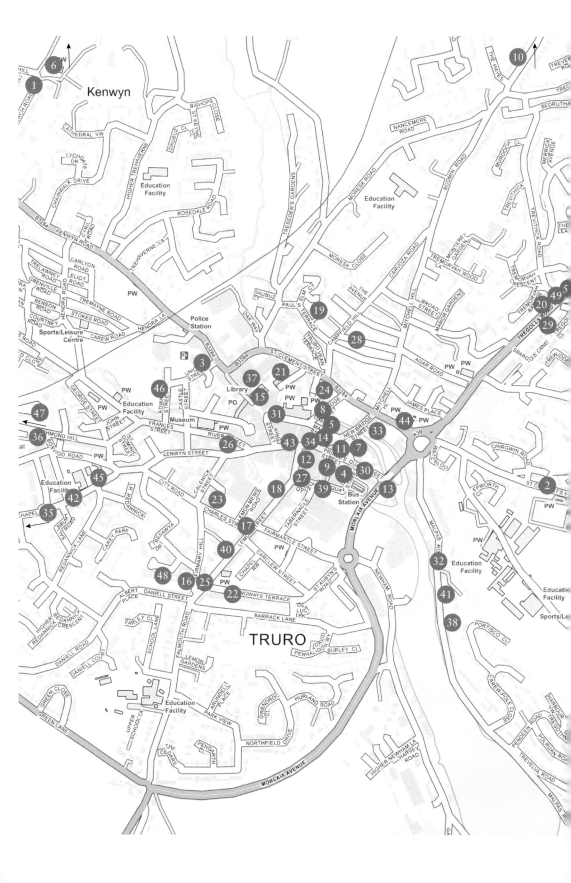

Key

1. Kenwyn Church
2. St Clement Church
3. Williams Court
4. Royal Bank of Scotland
5. Old Grammar School
6. Epiphany House
7. Old Mansion House
8. The Brick House
9. Princes House
10. Penmount
11. Frank & Caffin
12. Mansion House
13. Britannia Inn
14. Santander
15. Assembly Rooms
16. Royal Cornwall Hospital
17. Lemon Street Market
18. The Royal
19. Friends Meeting House
20. Alverton
21. Truro Methodist Church
22. Strangways Terrace
23. Walsingham Place
24. St Mary's Sunday School
25. Lander Monument
26. Royal Cornwall Museum
27. Municipal Buildings
28. Cornish's Beer Shop
29. Truro Union
30. Palace Buildings
31. Truro Cathedral
32. Trennick Mill
33. Furniss's Arch
34. Coinage Hall
35. Dalvenie House
36. The Railway Station
37. Library
38. Truro Swimming Club
39. The Pannier Market
40. The Plaza
41. Cricket Pavilion
42. County Hall
43. The Co-op
44. Roman Catholic Church
45. Baptist Church
46. Courts of Justice
47. Truro College
48. Truro Health Park
49. Waitrose
50. Trevethow Riel

Introduction

What does the name Truro mean? 'Three roads' or 'three rivers' has been suggested, but no one is quite sure. It is now generally accepted that Truro grew up in a valley between three rivers: the Kenwyn, the Allen and the Glasteinen. One of the oldest parts of town is the Victoria Square and Kenwyn Street area, where from the mid-thirteenth century until the Dissolution of the Monasteries the friary of the Dominicans once stood. The lovely old cross outside the west door of the cathedral in High Cross dates from those times. Despite being lost for some years, it was found under St Nicholas Street and restored to its rightful place. Truro still has part of the old parish church incorporated into the cathedral and some elegant town houses that have survived the test of time. The loss of the Red Lion in 1967 is still keenly felt by local people. At one time a row of properties known as Middle Row ran through the centre of what is now Boscawen Street, but once cleared away (with the loss of the old Guildhall) Truro became an elegant town with a wide front street. The pillars of the Guildhall now adorn the City Inn in Pydar Street and the stone tablet from it – urging vendors not to cheat – is safely tucked in under the Municipal Buildings.

The railway came to Truro from the other side of the Tamar in 1859 and opened up the county for trade and tourists. In 1877, Truro was granted city status, and the words of the brave horseback traveller Celia Fiennes in 1698 stating that it was a 'ruinated and disregarded place' seemed to belong to the past.

Truro is a port and once had many quays and boatbuilding businesses along the riverbank, which also had their ups and downs. Daniel Defoe visited in 1724 and said that Truro was 'sadly declining as a port'. Many of the changes of fortune to the town and port were as a result of the vagaries of the mining industry.

After the changes that came with the Second World War, the townspeople were lucky that not all the old buildings were swept away in the name of progress. Although Bodmin had held the assize courts, Truro and its County Hall gradually became the county's administrative centre – these days it has the law courts as well.

Many things have helped shape our town. Miners' riots in times of famine, wealthy mining adventurers building their town houses in better times, visits from John and Charles Wesley, the granting of city status and the building of a cathedral in the heart of the town have all helped to make the Truro we know today.

The 50 Buildings

1. Kenwyn Church

Kenwyn Church is dedicated to St Keyne, a female saint. She and her ladies arrived there around a hundred years before St Augustine brought Christianity to this country and it became the parish church for Truro. When Bishop Bronescombe came in 1259 to dedicate

Kenwyn Church
tower in the winter
sunshine.

The door of Kenwyn Church adorned with white flowers.

the chapel of the Dominican friars in the area of Kenwyn Street and the Chapel of Our Lady in town, he also went to Kenwyn to rededicate the church there. Being so old, it had probably undergone some restoration or even rebuilding, and as the journey from Exeter was long and difficult the bishop was making sure that everything that needed dedicating or rededicating was done while he was here. The church we see today is mostly from the fourteenth and fifteenth centuries and stands within the city boundary, although the parish of Kenwyn spreads way beyond this. The fact that it was a long uphill walk to the church was a problem for many people, so gradually the chapel of Our Lady (St Mary's Church) became their regular place of worship. The lychgate at Kenwyn has a slate-hung room. It was probably once used as a schoolroom, then in later years it was the Sunday school room as well as the venue for parish parties and cups of tea. In winter, when the leaves have fallen from the trees, it is easy to see the clock on the tower. It has a red face and looks cheerful even on the dullest of days.

St Keyne is the same lady who has a well near Liskeard named after her. The idea that the first one of a newly married couple to drink from the well will be the chief partner in the marriage is associated with it, but was the well anything to do with St Keyne herself? Probably not.

2. St Clement Church

St Clement Church was an alternative to Kenwyn Church for people who lived in the parish, which extended out as far as St Erme and covered the Mitchell Hill area of Truro with the River Allen being the boundary. Being down by the river there was a long walk to

The old stocks are safely stored in the church porch.

The only part of St Clement Church currently not covered in scaffolding.

get to the church, and much later the Church of St Paul was built as a chapel of ease. The earls of Cornwall lived at Condurrow before the Norman Conquest and would have had a chapel there. It is believed that St Clement Church was built on the site of an older chapel and was dedicated in 1249 – ten years before the intrepid Bishop Bronescombe arrived in 1259. The Ignioc Stone is a feature of St Clement and is inscribed with the words '*Vitali Fili Torrici*', which translates as 'Vitalus son of Torricus'. It used to stand in the vicarage drive but was moved to the churchyard in 1938, and is scheduled as an ancient monument. The beautiful church is currently undergoing restoration with Heritage Lottery funding. It is good to know that this church is being cared for and saved for future generations.

3. Williams Court

Henry Williams was a draper and a very public-spirited man who lived in Truro in the late 1500s. He was often asked to be a godfather as he was well known for his generosity; in fact, some people believed that he was mentally deficient as he gave away so much. As an old man in his seventies there was a rumour that his neighbour and one of his servants had forced him to remarry a much younger woman after his first wife died. It was suggested that he was kept indoors as he was a 'lunatic' and they hoped to benefit from his fortune. A letter was written by Geoffrey Bray to three of the most influential men in Cornwall – Sir William Killigrew, Francis Godolphin and Francis Basset – asking that Henry Williams' plight be looked into.

His will in 1629 was as generous as ever. He left £100 so that some money could be lent to any poor workmen of Truro. He also provided almshouses for twelve poor people to be built on the north-east side of Pydar Street with a meadow so they could have a cow to give them fresh milk. He made sure their clothes would be of a reasonable quality by stipulating that the fabric should cost 6s and 8d a yard. They were also to have the rindings (bark from the trees, presumably to burn for warmth) from Bishops Wood and 2s a week. The old almshouses were cleared away in the 1970s and the site used for council offices; the bungalows on the other side of the road have taken their place. Unfortunately, when the old almshouses were knocked down a memorial stone was taken away with the rubbish, which now stands in a car park near Newquay. A strange tale indeed, but Henry Williams was highly thought of and the modern bungalows in Union Street are his legacy today.

One of the 1970s bungalows that replaced the old almshouses.

The council offices built on the site of the original almshouses.

4. Royal Bank of Scotland

The Royal Bank of Scotland occupies an old and special building known as the Great House. It is believed to have been built by a member of the Gregor family, possibly a relative of the grandfather of Samuel Enys of the Old Mansion House. If so, this would date it to the later years of the 1600s. It has had many occupants over the years including the Hussey family, Mr Gwatkin of Killiow and Sir Francis Basset, but is well known in Truro as the town house of the Rosewarne family. Local historian Richard Polwhele lived there for a while in 1834 and describes the lavish interior that was the work of Rosewarne: mahogany and marble were the order of the day, with much ornamentation as was the fashion at the time. He was the MP for Truro and entertained lavishly in his spacious house. By the mid-1800s Henry Sewell Stokes lived there. He was an attorney by profession but had many other facets to his character. He was mayor of Truro in 1833, town clerk in 1856, the first clerk to the county council, and also a poet. He went to school with Dickens and

Above: The Royal Bank of Scotland, once the town house of the Rosewarne family.

Below: The side of the bank in the snow.

was sought as a friend by Tennyson, who used to come to Truro and stay in the Great House. Apparently, Tennyson – Poet Laureate at the time – wrote part of 'In Memoriam' there. The building is remembered by old Truronians today as Oscar Blackford the printers. Blackford's held the property from the late 1800s. Records from this time state that the house's original dining room had become a large shop and that there were at least fifteen rooms. There was a disastrous fire in the 1920s and half the building was lost, but it was still large enough for the printers to carry on.

5. Old Grammar School

Walter Borlase is credited with starting a school for boys in the church porch in St Mary's Street in 1549. It is possible that some sort of a school already existed with the rector of the church, Richard Fosse, acting as master. The building we see today was in use from around 1700 and specialised in the classics, with many of its pupils going on to Oxford.

The Old Grammar School still standing in St Mary's Street.

Truro Grammar School was known as the Eton of Cornwall and had many scholars who later became famous: Humphry Davy, inventor of the miners' safety lamp (among many other things), became president of the Royal Society; Edward Pellew became Lord Exmouth; Bishop Colenso; Richard and John Lander, famous for their expeditions to Africa; and the satirist Samuel Foote. During the headmastership of George Conan (who had come down from Westminster School in 1729) it was not unusual for Foote to visit his old school and promptly give the boys a day off – much to Conan's annoyance. Among other pupils were Henry Martyn, who was a missionary and translated the Bible into several languages, and Goldsworthy Gurney, who invented limelight and developed some early steam-powered carriages used to transport passengers across the country.

In 1906, the school moved to Cathedral Close on being taken over by the dean and chapter of the cathedral, but has now ceased to exist. The old building fell into decline when it was used as an ironmongers and later as a plumber's store. Fortunately, in 1947 the paint company Walpamur chose it to be their first depot in the county and set about restoring this lovely old building. They obtained a copy of the school's coat of arms from 1730 and had the plaster cast made that now adorns the north wall of the schoolroom. They were justifiably proud of their achievement and welcomed people to go and look for themselves. Today it is well used as a restaurant.

The restaurant has umbrellas should anyone wish to eat outside.

6. Epiphany House

There has been a building on this site since 1570. Despite much rebuilding 200 years after this, some of the original remains. It was the vicarage for Kenwyn until 1877 and had the distinction that John Wesley visited the house in 1787 on one of his many journeys to Cornwall. When Truro became a cathedral city the vicarage was promoted to the residence of the bishop. It was named Lis Escop, which is Cornish for 'Court of the Bishop'. It was to remain the home of the bishops until 1953. The first bishop was Edward White Benson, who oversaw some changes to the building as it needed enlarging to be a comfortable family home. It was in 1883 that the second bishop arrived, George Howard Wilkinson. He came from a parish in London where he had help with parish duties from a group of religious ladies who decided to come to Cornwall with him. They became the Community of the Epiphany and Alverton became their convent.

Epiphany House played a part in both world wars: in the First World War it was used as a convalescent home for officers and also housed Belgian refugees, and in the Second World War Bishop Hunkin used the grounds for fire-watching.

From 1953 to 1982 Epiphany House was used as part of the Cathedral School and was bought by them. A gift from the Copeland family in memory of their son Geoffrey, a former pupil, enabled the purchase and the name of the house was changed to Copeland Court.

The entrance to Epiphany House.

The ornate roofline at the front of Epiphany House.

As the school closed in 1982, the house became a convent for the Community of the Epiphany until 2001. These days Epiphany House can be contacted for quiet days, retreats and ways to serve the local community – just as the sisters had been doing.

7. Old Mansion House

In 1706, Samuel Enys inherited a house and a fortune from his grandfather, Henry Gregor. He also inherited a fortune from his other grandfather, also named Samuel Enys. By this time he had shares in many mines, was involved with a new system of smelting, had bought the manors of Kenwyn and Truro, and decided that he needed to live in a house that matched up to his standing in the town. In 1707, he built a house that is now known as the Old Mansion House on the site of his grandfather's former home. It had its own quay at the back where any goods required in his mining and smelting works could be unloaded.

The Old Mansion House with plaster covering Enys's prized bricks.

He made a very unusual decision when planning what his new property would look like: he arranged for two rooms of the old house to be saved and not demolished with the rest of the property. It is not known for sure which rooms these are and as the building has been used as offices for many years, it is guesswork that possibly supplied the answer. Two of the rooms are not like the rest; they are adjoining and have similar cornices and shell motifs

A boundary stone marked with an 'E' for Enys.

in the corners. These are possibly the two special rooms. One of the things Enys was most proud of was the fact that he had his new house faced with bricks that he had shipped down specially from London. Brick houses are rare in Truro and as the front of the Old Mansion House has been plastered over for many years, its bricks are no longer visible. Enys was well known for looking out of the round window at the top of his house. It gave a view of the cockpit, so if anyone who owed him money was betting – particularly if they won – he was straight down the stairs and out of the door to collect his money.

8. The Brick House

It is very rare to see brick houses in Truro, but one still stands in Old Bridge Street that dates from the early 1700s, a similar date to the Old Mansion House. In the run-up to the building of the cathedral many houses and industrial properties around the old church had to be demolished to make way for the new building. One of these that survived the clearance was the corner house by the cross, owned by the borough. Most of the properties near the cross were either owned by the Robartes family or rented by them from the borough. The house in question was the property of the borough and known as either the 'Brick House' or the 'House by the Cross'. It managed to survive until the post office was under construction (designed by Silvanus Trevail), when it was demolished along with its neighbour, the Unicorn Inn. The Brick House that we can see today in Old Bridge Street managed to survive the cathedral clearances, though Church Row had several houses that were knocked down. The house was described as being near the Bear Inn in 1854,

The front door under the blocked window has a high letter box.

The Brick House, a rarity in Truro.

suggesting that it had previously been part of the Bear Inn's premises. However, as bricks were so expensive it seems a little strange that the houses close to or part of the premises of an inn were clad in this way.

9. Princes House

One of the grand houses in Princes Street is – not surprisingly – named Princes House. This property was built around 1739 for William Lemon. William came from a poor family in Germoe, but as he was a bright young man he soon rose to become the manager of a smelting works known as Chyandour. Thomas Newcomen came to Cornwall at his invitation and pumped Wheal Fortune with his new steam-powered engine.

The architect of Princes House was Thomas Edwards, who came from Greenwich and created a beautiful home for William and his heiress wife, Isabella Vibert. Inside, a sweeping staircase rises gradually to the first floor where the sumptuous plasterwork on the ceiling over the stairs can be seen in intricate detail. Being a religious man, it was known that William Lemon had a chapel (complete with an organ) incorporated into his home; however, after many years as offices rather than a family home it is no longer obvious where it would be. The room at the top of the stairs on the first floor is one possibility as it has a fine marble fireplace and two pillars, which seems to be a strange addition to a living room. It is possible that at one time they had flanked an altar. Like the other houses in the street, there would also have been a pleasant garden at the rear that ran down to the river.

A very richly decorated plaster ceiling above the stairs.

The porch on Princes House is a later addition.

William Lemon is said to have taken lessons from George Conan, the master at the grammar school, to improve on the education he received when young. The Lemon family's country house was at Carclew – another of Thomas Edwards' creations. The 'Great' Mr Lemon, as he was known, died in 1760 a baronet and a multimillionaire by today's standards.

10. Penmount

Penmount has been a crematorium since 1956 but had a chequered history prior to that. In 1745, the site was known as Penhellick Mur and its mansion house was purchased and occupied by Revd John Collins, who was the rector of Redruth. The house passed through several hands after that, the first being General William Macarmick, who was a Member of Parliament. He rebuilt the house and gave it the name it is known by today: Penmount.

Part of Penmount that now houses the books of remembrance.

An addition to the old house, now one of the chapels.

The General was a sociable man and during his time at Penmount he was known for his hospitality – high-born or low-born, all were welcome to enjoy his festivities. When General Macarmick left to become the Governor of Cape Breton, Nova Scotia, in 1787 the property changed hands again. At one time Mr Willyams, a large landowner in the area, wanted to sell it and announced that it would make an excellent asylum. This suggestion fell on deaf ears.

The most notable owners of the house were Edward Shippham Carus-Wilson and his wife, who bought it in the late nineteenth century and became the grandparents of one of Cornwall's most famous historians: Charles Henderson. Henderson had a first-class degree from Oxford, lectured on the history of Cornwall in Exeter and was a fellow of Corpus Christi. He researched a great deal and acquired a vast amount of knowledge, but unfortunately he died aged only thirty-three while on his honeymoon in Italy. His father continued to live at Penmount and died there eight years after the death of his son. These days it is not just a place of sadness but also of peacefulness with beautiful gardens and far-reaching views.

11. Frank & Caffin

In 1749, William Lemon leased this property from Lord Falmouth and rebuilt it. As he already owned Princes House it would not have been for his own use. The architecture is typical of Truro town houses, with dormer windows and an elegant doorway similar to that in David Jenkyn's town house, now part of the Santander building. During the 1800s the house was purchased from Lord Falmouth by a Mr Baynard, who sold it on within a few months to a Mr Carthew. The deeds of the property at that time tell us that the Cornwall Library had been housed there. Outside the building is another of Truro's treasures, the Penfold pillar box. This style of postbox was only made for a few years and this one would have been placed there sometime in the 1860s. This property is known by most Truronians as the solicitors Frank & Caffin despite them not having occupied the building for many years. It is currently unoccupied and to let.

Once a solicitor's office, this old building has the Penfold postbox outside.

12. Mansion House

In 1759, the architect Thomas Edwards of Greenwich was again called upon to design a town house for a Truro family. Thomas Daniell, associate and later successor in business to William Lemon, intended to build a family home in Princes Street on a site known as Mount Fuddle. Daniell was thirty-nine years old, well established and had married the heiress Elizabeth Eliot, niece of a Cornishman from St Blazey, Ralph Allen. Allen was known as 'the Man of Bath' and had amassed a fortune by improving the postal service. His wedding present to his niece was enough Bath stone to face the new house – he owned quarries at Coombe Down. If the Bath stone had not been gifted to them it would have been possible to obtain similar stone just a mile or two away from Mount Fuddle at Newham; however, it would have cost more to get the stone from Newham than it would have if it had been bought from Bath and shipped down to Truro. The estimated cost of Mansion House was £8,500.

Thomas Edwards moved with the times. The plasterwork and decorations in the house were just as lavish as in Princes House but much more delicate, which matched the modern trend. Like its neighbour Princes House, it was not overly large but was of a high quality. The gardens stretched down to the river at the rear, an essential highway for businessmen. Also at the rear of the house are two balconies, enabling the family to go out and view their gardens and see down to the river. The Bath stone was replaced by granite at ground level

The Mansion House with two magnificent camellia bushes outside.

Above: The back of the building has balconies that give a view of the river.

Below: Delicate plasterwork and an elegant staircase in the Mansion House.

where the kitchens were situated. Daniell was a good host and, especially in his later years, took great pleasure in entertaining and preparing the punch for his guests himself.

Today, estate agents fill the beautiful rooms, which have been lovingly restored by Millers. It must be a pleasure to work in such elegant surroundings.

13. Britannia Inn

The Britannia Inn we see today was built in 1762, but there was property on the site long before that. The land was owned by the mayor and Corporation, and in 1680 the property was owned by a man called James Hocroft. When Nicholas Pearce asked to build a house next door the council came up with a requirement that Pearce had to agree to: he had to build a hedge of stone that was 8 feet high and 10 feet wide and plant it with hedge plants. This was a massive hedge but as the house he wanted to build was on land reclaimed from the river, there was an ever-present threat of flooding. During the 1700s a long-term resident of Hocroft House was a lady called Elizabeth Donnithorne, who died in 1760. Her son was a sailor, so presumably not at home often, and when he returned the house to the Corporation it was in a very poor state.

The Britannia Inn on a snowy day. It used to have a skittles alley.

With the end house demolished, the Britannia now stands at the end of the row.

In 1762, the lease was granted to Thomas Daniell. He rebuilt it and it became an attractive property overlooking the Green and the river at the rear. It is probable that the beams inside were ship timbers as they were much sturdier than the usual beams found in Cornish houses. Although there have been many alterations to the interior over the years, the house itself has changed little. At one time the property next door was let to Dr Wolcott (the satirist Peter Pindar) free of charge as he was a friend of owner Thomas Daniell. By 1853 the Britannia was an inn and busy too being so close to the quay. It had a skittles alley next door and the Green was so named as it was a bowling green at the back of the inn. Since 1967 the Britannia has become the end property of the block as houses were cleared away for the construction of Morlaix Avenue.

14. Santander

By the late 1770s there was building work going on in Boscawen Street (although it was not named this at the time) close to where the war memorial stands today. The building that is now Santander was under construction in 1775 and was owned by David Jenkyn. He definitely had a grand house. According to the Truro Buildings Group book about Boscawen Street one of the rooms had a very fine plaster ceiling with the date '1776' on it, but unfortunately the ceiling is long gone. Records show that in 1797 the property was still owned by David Jenkyn. He also owned the house next door: the Cornish Bank. Later, in the early 1800s the building was described as a residence with seven bedrooms and the usual dining room, parlour etc. It was definitely on quite a grand scale. The house was still

The home of the owner of the Cornish Bank.

The door that was known to all as Cannon & Collins' door.

described as being next to the Cornish Bank. For many years the beautiful doorway was the entrance to the chemists Cannon & Collins. The people of Truro have always been proud of the doorway, although more so when they were able to use it to go into the shop. These days it is not in use for the public. Today, after many years as the Abbey National Building Society, the building is home to Santander. Another chemist was also in residence here prior to Mr Cannon's occupation, so the change back to a bank is surprising. Would David Jenkyn recognise it as a descendant of his bank? Perhaps he would, although it is totally unlike anything he would have known.

15. Assembly Rooms

By the late 1700s Truro had become such a fashionable town that it was decided they should emulate other places such as Bath and have an assembly room for entertainments. Many of the leading families stayed in town for the winter and enjoyed the social life on offer. Today only the façade of the Assembly Rooms survives, decorated with the well-loved Wedgewood plaques. Thalia is at the top with Garrick and Shakespeare below. The money to fund the building of such an elegant addition to the town was raised by tontine. The cost of a share was £55 and Lord Falmouth bought three shares. The other twenty-five shares were sold on

The façade of the Assembly Rooms with plaques by Wedgewood.

a one-share-per-person basis. The shareholders were each required to nominate a life and as long as that person lived the shareholder had a stake in the business. The rooms opened in 1789 with no less a person than the famous actress Sarah Siddons present. In 1810, it was noticed that the shareholders had forgotten to nominate a life, so that was soon remedied. A man called John James nominated his five-year-old granddaughter Eliza, who was still alive 100 years after the rooms had opened. In 1889, Eliza inherited it all, although by that time new rooms had opened in the Palace Buildings. In 1806, a music festival was held with a performance of the Messiah followed by a ball. The Messiah was to be held in the church and tickets were 7s. Truro was so packed for the event that it was difficult for patrons to find a bed for the night. In 1815, a dinner was held in the Assembly Rooms to celebrate the return of General Vivian from the Battle of Waterloo, and over the years the venue played host to many balls and musical evenings. For many years the elegant building had sunk to being used as a garage being reinvented as a bakers – first it was one of Blewett's bakery shops and today it is Warrens.

Thalia, Garrick and Shakespeare above the Assembly Rooms.

16. Royal Cornwall Hospital

Accidents occur all the time but in the 1700s it was the frequency and horror of mining accidents that caused thoughts to turn to the need for a hospital in Cornwall. Three great public-spirited men – Sir Francis Basset, Sir John St Aubyn and Sir William Lemon – set about making the hospital a reality. The closest newspaper to Cornwall was the *Sherborne Mercury*, and on 20 May 1799 it announced that the building of Cornwall General Infirmary was complete. It was a twenty-bed establishment and the first house surgeon appointed was Dr Hector Bull, who held the post for fifty-five years.

In 1809, the Royal Cornwall Infirmary (so named as the patron was the Prince of Wales) acquired the assets and estate of the manor of Ponteboy along with the lazar house of St Lawrence in Bodmin. This provided a source of income for the hospital but came with an obligation to care for any lepers that might need attention. In previous centuries the leper house in Truro was in the area of Chapel Hill and Parkvedras Terrace. It was a short distance from the feature in the old wall of the hospital known as the leper's arch. In medieval times lepers passed through the arch to the lazar house.

Patients were admitted to the hospital with a letter from a subscriber. Wealthy people were attended to at home, but as hospital facilities improved the wealthy were seen to be at a disadvantage. In 1878, an outbreak of typhoid at the hospital carried off the surgeon's wife. The sewer ran past the building in Infirmary Hill but was not connected to it.

The nurses' home (now demolished) behind the leper's arch.

A side of the hospital not usually photographed, showing the variety of windows.

In August 1942 the hospital was hit by German bombs, resulting in loss of life to staff, patients and visitors. Much of its work was transferred to Treliske in 1966 and today the building is known by the name of the architect William Wood and houses modern flats in its familiar exterior.

17. Lemon Street Market

The elegant street of houses that make up Lemon Street grew up piecemeal from around 1800 with no thought of town planning. What is now Lemon Street Market was once stabling for one of the grand houses but in the 1920s or 1930s it was bought by S. Hicks & Son, who already had garage premises in River Street that ran through to Kenwyn Street. William Hicks (the 'Son') had a turntable installed so cars could be turned onto Lemon Street rather than reversing and causing a hazard. The building was bought from Walter Hitchens, who had run his stabling business there. Leading to the market's entrance the arrangement of the stones on the pathway can be seen, where the large oblong slabs could accommodate the wheels of a carriage. Shops and cafés (one upstairs and one downstairs) tempt the customers in today. The turntable was moved and revamped when Viv and Simon Hendra upgraded the market a few years ago; tables and chairs are now set out on

This arch led to the mews for some Lemon Street houses.

The entrance to Lemon Street Market with shops and cafés inside.

it in the lower café. After the parade of lanterns that is normally held just before Christmas each year, a selection of the lanterns are hung from the ceiling of the building – it was not unusual to see an elephant or tiger floating above the upstairs café. Although Viv Hendra has since moved on to other things and is no longer sitting at his computer surrounded by artwork, it is where many a painting of old Truro has been discovered. The old stables have today been transformed into an attractive working business.

18. The Royal

In 1804, a hostelry called the King's Head was newly built and listed for sale by its then occupier, Miss Husband. The accompanying advertisement made much of its situation as being in the new street close to the river (Lower Lemon Street), the extensive range of rooms and the fact that stabling was close by. In 1806, Mr Pearce from Redruth bought it, renamed it Pearce's Hotel and decorated it in an elegant style. He advertised that the mail coach called the *Quicksilver* called every day on the way to London, and also that it was possible to reach Plymouth every other day by taking the coach to Torpoint. The hotel became very important in the life of Truro as Mr Pearce catered for all manner of occasions. Business meetings were often held there (especially those

The Royal Hotel in Lower Lemon Street is as popular as ever.

Mannings Restaurant is a part of the Royal Hotel.

concerned with mining) and dinners, both private and part of the civic life of the town, were regular events. In 1832, a dinner was held in honour of Lord Boscawen's coming of age; in 1834, almost fifty members of the clergy sat down to dinner with the Bishop of Exeter after attending a service in the parish church; and in 1835 Mr Pearce managed the lying-in-state of Lord de Dunstanville on his way home to Tehidy.

As the hotel was in a busy part of town there were often accidents outside. One occurred in 1840 when a horse was startled coming out of Pearce's Yard and ran off the quay and into the river. The driver of the market cart jumped out and a coachman jumped into the river; the coachman was injured but the horse was unscathed.

It was in 1846 that the name of the hotel was changed to The Royal to mark the occasion of a visit from Prince Albert. Although Queen Victoria was with him, she chose to stay on board the royal yacht, which was moored at Malpas. The royal coat of arms is over the door and Mannings Restaurant – a part of the building – is popular for meals.

19. Friends Meeting House

In 1825, a meeting house for the Society of Friends – otherwise known as Quakers – was opened for worship in the presence of a large crowd. The highlight of the meeting was the presence of Mrs Elizabeth Fry and her sister. Elizabeth Fry was a well-known prison reformer and her address was eagerly awaited. The meeting house had been built with money raised by local people and the name most connected with the effort was William Tweedy. He had been employed at Somerset House in London but had been given the opportunity to come to Cornwall and be responsible for the Cornish Bank. It was in 1802 that he arrived with his family to live at Truro Vean – now called Benson House. Following his wife's example, eight years after her admission to the Society of Friends, Tweedy became a Quaker in 1817, adopting their style of dress and becoming an Elder of the meeting. Tweedy had the meeting house built in the bottom corner of his garden at a cost of just under £1,500. To the side of the building is a graveyard with rows of plain slate footstones and a peaceful air.

The previous building on the site of the meeting house would have been the carpet factory. This had been a beacon of forward thinking at the time as people with disabilities were employed so that they had a chance to earn a living and provide for themselves.

During the Second World War evacuees from Stoke Damerel High School in Plymouth used the meeting house. Their headmistress accompanied them, being a member of the Plymouth Meeting. By the late 1970s the house was becoming dilapidated and a decision was taken to restore and modernise it. It is still in use today.

The Friends Meeting House in spring sunshine.

The quiet graveyard behind the Meeting House.

20. Alverton

In 1830, William Tweedy of the Cornish Bank had the east wing of Alverton built. He intended Alverton to be a family home but opened the gardens to the public so they could be enjoyed by all. His interest in gardens was such that he became the president of the Royal Horticultural Society. Upon his death in 1859 the house was partly owned by the Bank of Cornwall. The gardens were open for another ten years, but in 1879 the bank failed and the house (by this time known as Alverton Manor) was sold. It was in 1883 that £3,000 was paid to Sir John Protheroe Smith and Alverton Manor became the property of the sisters of the Order of the Epiphany. They immediately started building the chapel; it was lovingly looked after and had beautiful stained-glass windows. On the occasions when St Paul's Church was undergoing repair, the congregation went to the nuns' chapel for their services. Today the chapel is known as the Great Hall and the building was converted into a hotel when the nuns moved to Epiphany House in 1984. It is now known as the Alverton.

Above: The Great Hall at Alverton that was the chapel of the convent.

Below: The clock tower and part of the building not seen from the front.

21. Truro Methodist Church

Before the Methodists had a church of their own, from around 1795 they used a room near the West Bridge (Victoria Square) for their meeting place. After some time a plot of land nearby became available. A Methodist member named Mark Rowe gave the land and a small chapel was built. By the time he died it had already been extended twice, so the hunt was still on for larger premises. The Methodist fraternity were not popular at this time and it became difficult to obtain the land they needed. When John Vivian died his son put the house in Pydar Street (now Union Place) up for sale and it was snapped up by the Methodists just before someone else offered to buy it. The chosen architect was Philip Sambell, the deaf and mute son of a timber merchant who left Truro with many elegant buildings. The building cost £3,990, the foundation stone was laid in 1829, and the church opened in 1830. The building work was scrutinised by the seven trustees, who took their task so seriously that they would gather several times a week at 6 a.m.

The site on which the chapel stands has an interesting history. The houses in that area had large gardens and behind the Vivian's house was an old orchard that produced apples called Cornish Gilliflowers. These apples were a favourite of George III and every year some were sent up to London for him.

Today, the Methodist Church has a café where members of the congregation or the public can sit and have a tea or coffee and some cake. The café is called Sambell's after the silent hard-working man who designed such an elegant building.

Truro Methodist Church with Sambell's café open for business.

Improvements to Pydar Street opened up a good view of the Methodist Church.

22. Strangways Terrace

Strangways Terrace is an elegant row of large houses that leads off the top of Lemon Street and looks down over the town. The buildings that were demolished on the site were the barracks that came down in 1835. It would seem that it took little effort to take down the barracks as they were not built well; in fact, as soon as they were erected bits of walls were blown down in the wind and a large piece of roof flew away. They were designed for 180 men and horses. The men's quarters gave them no protection from the cold or weather, so they often preferred to sleep in the stables with the horses. By 1837 the first of the houses designed by Philip Sambell was leased, with the only reminder of the former barracks being the name of the road behind them – Barrack Lane.

Strangways Terrace seems to have been the ideal place to start a school – possibly because of the size of the properties. In 1880, Truro College opened its doors to pupils. It was a Wesleyan boarding school and is known today as Truro School. The foundation stone of the new building was laid in 1881. The school moved to the current premises in 1882 and the clock tower overlooks the town. It is easy to forget that the school has grown considerably over the years. In 1897, a boarding school for girls was moved from Strangways Terrace and became the High School for Girls, and the County Grammar School for girls was started in the Terrace in 1906.

Above: A view of Strangways Terrace from the health park.

Below: Some of the smart houses built on the site of the barracks.

23. Walsingham Place

Although no one is certain, it would seem that Walsingham Place is another of Philip Sambell's classical creations that gives Truro an air of elegance. Edmund Turner had Walsingham Place built. Walsingham was a family name of the Turners, which could explain why it was chosen. Edward was the Member of Parliament for Truro and died unexpectedly at his son-in-law's home in London in 1848. Now used as offices, these unusual houses were once family homes, although there is a suspicion that in some properties a gentleman could tuck his mistress away out of sight!

During the Second World War many Americans were camped near Truro and had every modern convenience. When Truro housewives heard about their washing machines, flushing toilets (despite being camped in tents) and electric light they decided to campaign for better living conditions for themselves.

After the war, aware that Truro needed modernising, the city council wished to sweep all the old buildings away and start again. Fortunately, Sir John Betjeman was aware of what was likely to happen and came to Truro himself. Apparently he was seen poking the mayor in the chest declaring that the demolition of Walsingham Place could not be allowed to happen; it was a treasure to be preserved. The council saw sense and realised that modernisation could take place without losing all the old parts of the city.

As one walks up Walsingham Place from Victoria Square it is interesting to note that the doors on the left have rather friendly-looking lion heads above, while the decoration above the doors on the right are fan-shaped leaves.

Walsingham Place, which was rescued from ruin by John Betjeman.

Friendly lions stand guard over the doorway.

24. St Mary's Sunday School

In 1835, construction began on a building for a Sunday school in Old Bridge Street. It was originally a Sunday school for the parish of St Mary's, as can be seen from the inscription over the door. Then, in 1841, a survey revealed that many children received no schooling at all and so a day school for boys was started in the following year. It was another seven years before a school for girls was started.

The building suffered a bad fire in 1891 that gutted the interior and was believed at the time to be the work of an incendiary. When the caretaker had finished cleaning the rooms she discovered her keys were missing and so, knowing there was to be a Coal Club meeting later that evening, she left the door unlocked. At the end of the meeting all was still in order, but sometime later the fire raged through the building and the fire brigade was sent for. They attended quickly, but the damage was done; the inside of the building was gutted.

More recently the former school has been a café, and it is now a home interiors shop.

St Mary's Sunday School and the old medieval bridge.

25. Lander Monument

The Lander Monument, which commemorates Richard Lander, is situated at the top of Lemon Street and gazes down over the city. Lander was born in the Fighting Cocks Inn in 1804. Living close to one of the many quays that sat along the riverbank as a youngster, he spent time with the sailors and learned about their foreign travels. He also spent time in the West Indies as a servant to a merchant and later ventured to the Cape of Good Hope, but he is best remembered for his travels in Africa on the River Niger.

Richard Lander on his monument braving the storm.

Another view of Lander showing he has had some repair work.

In 1832 Richard and John Lander were entertained at a dinner to celebrate their adventures and money was raised with the intention of giving them something as a memento. Unfortunately Richard died on his next expedition and as John wished for a more lasting tribute, more money was raised for a column, which was designed by Philip Sambell. After much deliberation the decision was made to build the monument at the top of Lemon Street.

The money they had raised so far was enough for the statue and they decided to spend what was left on making the column taller, without considering the danger of altering the architect's plan. In 1835 Richard's daughter led the procession up Lemon Street for the laying of the foundation stone and the band played 'Rule Britannia'. However, in 1836 the column, which was now almost complete, fell with a crash that shook the street. They now had to raise more funds and start again! Finally, after nearly twenty years and with costs rising all the time, the statue by Neville Northey Burnard was placed on the column and now gazes down over Truro.

26. Royal Cornwall Museum

Philip Sambell was born in Devonport in 1798 and came to Truro in 1822 when his father had a timber yard in Fairmantle Street. Philip was deaf and mute but was still educated to such a standard that he became a much-respected architect.

The Baptist Chapel incorporated into the museum is now a café and art shop.

The building known today as the Royal Cornwall Museum was designed by Sambell as a savings bank in 1845. There was an article in the *West Briton* that enthused about the new building, which it claimed would to be an excellent addition to the town, though remarked that Truro was sadly lacking in architectural elegance. The granite-faced building has both Ionic and Doric columns, and steps rising to the entrance portico. It is as smart today as it was when it was built.

As a result of a slump in the mining trade attempts were made to sell the building. By 1898 it was rented by Henderson's Mining School. Henderson was a Scotsman who had travelled the world working in the mining industry. He retired to Truro where he set up an educational establishment for miners who wished to learn to be mining managers. However, he died in 1903 and the building was sold to the Royal Institution of Cornwall, a society founded in 1818. They bought it for the princely sum of £1,800. The building next door to the museum was also one of Philip Sambell's designs and built as the Baptist Chapel. For many years the cricket club held their annual service in the Baptist Chapel and then crossed River Street to have a slap-up lunch in the Imperial Hotel. For many years now this building has been an annex of the museum. A café now joins the two buildings and spills over to the old chapel, which also houses a craft and art shop.

The entrance to the museum with the attractive flower beds outside.

27. Municipal Buildings

The Municipal Buildings is an Italianate structure in the middle of Boscawen Street. It was designed by the architect Christopher Eales and was built in 1846–47. Today it has many uses and houses the Tourist Information Centre on the ground floor, a useful calling point for visitors to the town looking for directions, lodgings or even a local postcard and souvenir. Outside the Information Centre, sheltered under the arches, is a venue for flea markets and craft stalls. How many stallholders realise they are operating under the Jenkin Daniell stone? This tablet was once in the old Market House, which stood at the end of Middle Row with a butcher's shop below at street level and the council chamber above. The tablet reads: 'Who seks to find eternal tresure must use no guile in waight or mesure Jenken Daniel Maior 1615.'

The Hall for Cornwall is situated upstairs in part of the Municipal Buildings, with its entrance on Back Quay. It has rooms to rent for functions. The front of the building houses council offices. At the top of the flight of granite stairs, the room on the right is designated as the Town Hall. Until comparatively recently it was full of uncomfortable wooden seating as it had been the Magistrates' Court. Until 1921 the police station was also located in the Municipal Buildings, so officers presumably did not have far to go to keep an eye on the revellers leaving the Saturday night dances held in the building. At times it also housed a

Municipal Buildings housing the Tourist Information Centre.

The flag is flying ready for St Piran's Day.

skating rink, pantomimes, fashion shows and was the site of the Regal Cinema in the 1930s and 1940s. It was well used by amateur operatic and dramatic societies and was the venue for many school speech days – the trick was to make sure you were not sitting behind one of the many pillars that blocked a view of the stage. In 1914, the clock tower caught fire and fell into the council chamber. The old clock had a black face whereas the replacement is white.

28. Cornish's Beer Shop

In 1847, Richard Cornish had a beer shop in what was then Factory Lane – now Campfield Hill. In 1848, an inquest was held there into the death of a young man called John Tresize who was working for Cornwall Railway. Instead of using the skip to take him to the top of the shaft in which he was working, he stepped onto a barrel that was the counterweight. The barrel slipped and Tresize plunged to the bottom and was killed.

The Cornish's beer shop, also known as the Miners Inn.

Inset: The building was protected by fire badge No. 425573 should a fire occur.

In 1849/50 William Harvey took over the premises and changed the name to the Miners Inn. He often allowed drinking out of hours – even on a Sunday – and while Constable Woolcock knew this happened, he was not able to gain entry to the house; however, he did discover Mrs Harvey letting drinkers out of the back door. When Harvey died in 1858, friends of his – miners from Chacewater – persuaded the priest heading the funeral to delay the service to 5.15 p.m. They used the extra time to parade around the town with the corpse and a rackety brass band, shouting hymns in a non-musical fashion. They upset evensong with their loud behaviour and threatened the priest with violence when he asked for the names of the ringleaders – fortunately he managed to escape into a back lane. It was all colourfully reported in the local press. Harvey's wife decided to sell up in 1860 and the licence was not renewed. The house is now a respectable private residence named Chartwell and has the distinction of a fire badge affixed to the front of the property. It seems that one of the owners paid for private fire cover in the days before modern fire brigades. Hopefully, if there had been a fire, the horse-drawn engine would have arrived in time for the men to put it out.

29. Truro Union

The Poor Law Amendment Act of 1834 changed the system whereby parishes were expected to care for their destitute residents. All parishes had a workhouse to care for these poor souls. It was known that if a destitute person did not belong to the parish where they asked for help they would be sent to the parish responsible for them. The law stated that Poor Law unions were to be formed that could care for more people and relieve the burden on the individual parishes. As the Truro Union Workhouse was not built and ready

New apartments were built in the style of the original building.

Now full of comfortable apartments, the outside of Truro Union is forbidding.

for occupants until 1851, the parish workhouses were still in use but run by the Poor Law Guardians. These were people who were elected each year and met regularly to oversee their duties. When the Truro Union opened in 1851 there were 134 inmates. In recent years, the signpost bearing the words 'Truro Union' that pointed across the top of Bodmin Road to Tregolls Road has unfortunately disappeared.

Jobs inside the workhouse were hard: picking oakum (strands of fibres used in caulking boats) would cut the fingers, and the heavy work of breaking stones was no better. In 1877, however, we know that the inmates had something to look forward to at Christmas. The board of guardians provided the money for each inmate to have a dinner of roast beef, plum pudding for desert and a pint of beer. Seventy-two people sat down to the feast.

Part of the building was used as a hospital during the First World War. In 1929, the board of guardians was disbanded and with them went the outdated workhouse system. The building served as the Isolation Hospital for many years, and later as NHS offices. Today it has been converted into flats and apartments, but traces of the old workhouse can still be seen here and there, such as the granite cantilevered staircases with iron bannisters.

30. Palace Buildings

In 1867, the foundation stone was laid for the new public rooms known as the Palace Buildings. Truro had outgrown the classical building at High Cross and it was thought that rather than lag behind other Cornish towns such as Camborne and Penzance, new rooms

The Palace Buildings used to be for leisure purposes but now contains businesses.

should be built. The rear of the building looks onto the Green, an area that has completely changed in character from what it was in the heyday of the Palace Buildings. The Green was a bowling green then, but had many other uses too as there was always room for a crowd to gather. Prospective parliamentarians were allowed to address the masses, troops could be drilled and occasionally there was a fair or exhibition to enjoy.

The building is in the Gothic style favoured by the Victorians and still makes a statement. Some of the other buildings in the row were demolished to make way for the new building, and in the 1960s adjacent property was demolished to allow Green Street to be widened. The Dolphin Inn came down too. It had previously been called the Fighting Cocks, which was derived from the fact that a cock pit had been on the site. The landlord had been John Lander, father of Richard and John Lander, who are famous for their explorations in Africa. All that remains today is a plaque on the wall, although the monument for Richard and John remains at the top of Lemon Street, looming over the town.

The Palace Buildings had many uses. It contained a concert hall with an organ, was the home of the Truro Philharmonic Society, the billiard club and the chess club met there, and it also contained a library. By the 1950s and '60s it was the home of a cinema. Youngsters could go to see a film and visit the Dolphin Buttery (on the site of the former Dolphin Inn) for soft drinks and cakes.

The back of the Palace Buildings faces the bus depot.

31. Truro Cathedral

In May 1880 the Prince and Princess of Wales arrived to lay the foundation stone of Truro Cathedral, the first cathedral to be built in the country since the sixteenth century. On their way into the new city they passed under Triumphal Arches designed by architect Silvanus Trevail, then went to Southleigh, Lemon Street, which had an interior decorated as

The cathedral rises from the heart of the town and towers over Cathedral Lane.

The west front of the cathedral at High Cross, on the site of the old church.

a Masonic lodge. The Prince of Wales laid the stone with ecclesiastical and Masonic rites, which was not to everyone's taste.

By 1910 the building was completed, but much had changed around the town since construction had started. Edward White Benson was the new bishop and had to overcome reluctance by some locals about the loss of their parish church, which had been dedicated by Bishop Bronescombe in 1259 and was dear to their hearts. Architect John Loughborough Pearson realised, however, that its south aisle could be saved and incorporated into the new building and act as a parish church. While building was in progress a wooden shed was also erected in High Cross. Bishop Benson devised the ceremony of Nine Lessons and Carols, which has since become a favourite worldwide, and was first performed in the wooden cathedral on Christmas Eve in 1880.

The cathedral is built of a variety of stones: Mabe granite and Bath stone are outside and softer granite, Bath stone, polyphant and serpentine, among others, are inside. The clock tower is clad in Cornish copper. In 1901, Mr Hawke Dennis of Redruth paid for the 244-foot-high central tower known as the Victoria Tower, and in 1910 Mrs Hawkins of Trewithen gave the money for the two western towers, Edward and Alexandra. The organ is a Henry Willis, with a Byfield in the south aisle. There are many dedications, including John and Charles Wesley in stained glass; Henry Martyn, a missionary who translated the Bible into Persian and Armenian; and the brother of Rector George Fitzpen (or Phippen), Owen Fitzpen, who was taken prisoner by Turks in 1620 and captive for seven years before fighting for release with ten other Christians.

The south aisle of the church within the cathedral.

32. Trennick Mill

The year 1864 saw various prominent members of the town writing a letter to the Town Clerk to suggest that a 'pleasure ground' would greatly benefit the people of Truro and be good for their health and well-being. The idea was that there should be plenty of room well away from the dust and dirt of the roads for youngsters to run around and play, room for others to take a walk or sit and admire the view, and also space for the militia to exercise. Nothing was done for many years but the park gradually took shape in the late 1800s. Lord Falmouth and the Duchy made sure that foreshore was available between Waterloo Quay and the mill stream, along with the stream to Sunny Corner. The mill stream that flowed through Trennick was known to be ancient, but no one knew its history for certain. The property known as the Mill House was sold in 1854. One of the companies invited to submit a plan for the new park was Robert Veitch of Exeter, whose idea incorporated a system of ponds and lakes that would have made use of the old mill stream. However, Veitch's plan was not accepted and the course of the mill stream was altered to accommodate the new pleasure grounds. The Mill House (now known as Trennick Mill) was subject to regular flooding but was a firm favourite with visitors to the park. At one time it was known as the Junket House. I believe this was because junket was served there, but it could also refer to the happy times people had in their new parkland. Today Trennick Mill is an ideal spot for a meal, a cream tea or a drink overlooking the park with its trees, flowers, play area and riverside walk. Next to Trennick Mill is a pond filled with ducks and swans and the walk around the pond is a good place to see all manner of birdlife.

The perfect place for refreshment near the park.

The mill overlooks the park full of daffodils and ducks.

33. Furniss's Arch

There were once days in Truro when the air was filled with tempting aromas. The Furniss biscuit and sweet factory perfumed the town with the smell of gingerbread, boiled sweets and peppermint rock. All that remains of the factory now is the archway in New Bridge Street that led to the building, but the memory of baking days lingers on. John Cooper Furniss was believed to have been born in Truro around 1834. By the time the cathedral was under construction his pasties, cakes and biscuits were very popular with the workmen. His bakery was originally in King Street, but by 1886 he had a tearoom in what was then called Church Lane, a very handy location for both the townspeople and the builders. Some of his customers were from the railway station, and he supplied the buffet for workers and passengers alike – pity the poor soul who had to push a handcart laden with bakery products all the way up Richmond Hill. When Furniss realised just how popular his products were, he formed a company in 1886 with Mr T. Chirgwin and Mr W. Bennett so

At one time this was the way to work for the staff of Furniss's company.

Looking down Furniss Close to the retirement flats.

he could expand his business. His new factory was on Duchy Wharf and was accessed via the archway we see today. When he died in 1888 he left 100 shares in the company so that the income from them could provide coal for needy citizens of Truro. The charity still exists today and is overseen by Truro City Council, but the number of needy people with coal fires has dwindled dramatically in these days of central heating. A trip to the factory was often the highlight of a school year, seeing the gingerbreads bobbing along a conveyor belt or the letters 'TRURO' being incorporated into a stick of rock. The company still exists but the factory has now relocated to Redruth.

34. Coinage Hall

In almost all the photos of Boscawen Street it is the nineteenth-century mock-Tudor building that dominates the picture. In 1351, the Duke of Cornwall instructed his staff to either buy or build a house for the coinage. This would have been important to him as

The Coinage Hall faces the war memorial and marks the site of Middle Row.

The side of the building has several styles of doors and windows.

one of his sources of revenue was the tax paid to the duchy when the ingots of tin were assayed. The site of the old coinage hall was at the end of Middle Row where the 'new' bank building is situated. These days the ground floor is a pizza restaurant and a long flight of stairs ascends to a Victorian-style coffee shop and an antiques shop. Halfway up the stairs is what appears to be a hole in the wall but is in fact another shop. In the days when the property was a bank, this was the vault. It was no good having a vault below the building as the river runs under the street. Outside the building, beside the taxi rank, stands an attractive old pump. It is the site of one of the town's pumps, but this one is much nicer to look at. The original pump was boarded in and so looked rather like a long, tall wooden box. It is still in use but has been moved to the cemetery, halfway up St Clement's Hill. The plaque on the wall near the pump commemorates John Wesley. He preached to the townsfolk when there were more people than would fit into the preaching house.

35. Dalvenie House

Dalvenie House was built for James Henderson, a Scottish mining engineer who took up residence with his wife and family – three sons and three daughters – in 1892. He was born in 1821 in Aberdeen and led an interesting life with several different careers. He worked in southern Australia as a government surveyor but returned to England in 1850, when he came to Cornwall to take charge of his father's mining businesses and to set up in business himself as a civil mining engineer, surveyor and mine agent. Other business interests included the making and storing of ice, and the invention of a surveying instrument named the Rapid Traverser. The building in River Street that is now the Royal Cornwall Museum was acquired by Mr Henderson when he needed to expand his School of Mining Engineering and Metallurgy. Its purpose was to educate miners who could already read and write to become mining engineers themselves. James Henderson also held many public offices, including that of captain of the Truro Fire Brigade, leader of the Truro Conservative Party, and he was elected mayor of Truro in 1902. Truro's beautiful Victoria Gardens were designed by him and opened in 1898 in celebration of the Queen's Diamond Jubilee. The house has been used as council offices for many years and prior to that was the boarding house of Truro High School for Girls. It has many original features, including the beautiful

Dalvenie House, close to the entrance to County Hall.

Dalvenie with part of the once extensive gardens.

glass of the inner door, quarry tiles in the hall and arched doorways. The quarry tiles are patterned in the main house, but are plain red and cream in the servants' quarters. The main staircase is much admired but there is a narrow spiral one for servants that leads to the attic. James Henderson died aged eighty-two in Dalvenie House in 1903.

36. The Railway Station

The railway came to Truro in various stages. The most significant was in 1877, when it was possible to travel from Paddington to Penzance, and the older branch line from Truro could carry passengers on to Falmouth. The Plymouth to Truro line and the Truro to Falmouth line were part of the Cornwall Railway, who used the broad 7-foot gauge tracks as favoured by Brunel. The Truro to Penzance line was part of the West Cornwall Railway and used standard gauge, which was known as narrow gauge at the time. In order for trains to run to Penzance an extra rail was laid beside the

Once horses and carts lined up at the station to deliver goods to town.

narrow gauge, meaning carriages that were either narrow or broad could use the rails – sometimes this could all be on the one train! The Great Western Railway took over in 1889, and by 1892 all the rails were standard gauge. It was after the takeover by the Great Western Railway that the railway station we see today was built. There had been one there before but it was often complained about for being dirty and draughty. The new station was opened in 1900. On 6 August 1942 two German planes dropped bombs on the City Hospital and strafed the railway station as they flew off. Bullet holes can still be seen in the footbridges, although as a result of time and paintwork they are not immediately obvious so need to be looked for. Several people lost their lives that day and on 6 August 2017 a small ceremony was arranged by Andy Pentecost (who lost a family member). Kingsley Wright laid a poppy wreath and the ceremony was watched by friends and members of Truro Old Cornwall Society in the waiting room on the up platform.

A modern entrance to the Victorian station.

37. Library

John Passmore Edwards was a local boy who made an outstanding life for himself. Born in Blackwater near Truro, he made a fortune in London as a publisher after working as a journalist in Manchester. He devoted much of his fortune to good works throughout the country, including funding hospitals, schools and libraries. In Truro, the library on the corner of Pydar Street and Union Place and the technical school at the far end of the building are the result of his generosity. He offered £2,000 to any town that built a library, and when Octavius Ferris, a Cornishman who had been the headmaster of a school in Manchester, left the princely sum of £10,000 to be divided between Penzance, Falmouth, Truro, Camborne and Redruth the scene was set.

Passmore Edwards laid the foundation stone in 1896. The chosen architect was local man Silvanus Trevail, who built it in what he called his Tudor Renaissance style in Plymouth

Above: The technical school educated many Truro boys until the age of fourteen.

Left: Once Truro City Library, it is now run by Cornwall Council.

limestone and Bath stone. The technical school specialised in teaching useful trades to boys and the curriculum included art, agriculture and science. There are wonderful carvings on the building. They are rather difficult to see, but have been beautifully executed and show a variety of trades. The library that had been Truro City Library and was governed by the city council was lost to them in the local government reorganisation in 1974; it is now run by Cornwall Council. It is bright and modern inside, still with the iconic Trevail architecture, and what was once a dreary reading room is now an attractive coffee lounge.

38. Truro Swimming Club

We know that Truro Swimming Club dates back to around 1910. It was a well-respected club and had many members. Truro boys often dived off Boscawen Bridge to swim, and much of the swimming club's activities were carried out close to the bridge on Worth's Quay. The lovely Victorian pavilion that graced the quay for so many years is now gone, but the boys once used it as a changing room when they had a special event. Every year, without fail, they had a gala day and crowds would come to watch and enjoy the scene. There was also a water polo team who played in the Cornwall league and travelled all over Cornwall for their matches. At one game in Truro, Kingsley Wright remembers the

The old swimming club hut, now refurbished and popular at Sunny Corner.

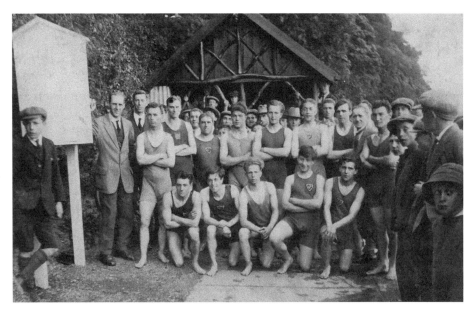

The members of the swimming club pose in their costumes around 1920.

goalie holding up something that had got washed into his net and asking the captain what he should do with it. It was a large water rat! Another thing they liked to do was to dive off the metal gantry attached to the coastlines building, and the day that John Pearn came up covered in mud is vividly remembered. When it was thought to test the water around Worth's Quay it was decided to move to Sunny Corner, where the water was cleaner. This was in 1953 and there was already a shelter there that the club used. The shelter has been recently refurbished and made into an attractive area. Some steps led down to the water and, depending on the amount of mud, it can be possible to see tiles on the riverbed. This was a tiled area around 10 feet by 20 feet where many youngsters learned to swim, but it was never a swimming pool. When walking to the refurbished shelter and seats today, one walks over a concreted area where a new changing room was built for the club in 1953.

39. The Pannier Market

The Pannier Market is still thought of by many as HTP, a company that once thrived there. Three men formed it in 1890. The 'H' is for W. Hosken & Son, who owned Loggans Mill at Hayle – the most modern mill in Cornwall at the time. They had been millers since 1800 and their flour was of the highest quality and in great demand. The 'T' was for John Harvey Trevithick, one of Richard Trevithick's sons. During the second half of the eighteenth century they became importers of grain and millers. The 'P' was for J. S. Polkinhorn of Kenwyn Street (he later moved his business to Malpas Road), who dealt in agricultural tools and also milled foodstuff for animals. HTP was a very well-known and respected company in Cornwall, and they had a staff of travelling salesmen to get around the county. Their transport was a pony and trap at first, but gradually motor cars were introduced. The need to maintain their fleet brought them into the motor trade and the large premises

Above: HTP on Back Quay.

Below: The Pannier Market with a selection of shops opens out onto the Piazza.

built for them in 1934 (now the Pannier Market) made keeping the vehicles under cover and having room to service them an easy task. They were also agents for Austin Tractors and later for Austin Motor (Co.). By 1934, this side of the business became HTP Motors Ltd. With the outbreak of the Second World War they handed over all their commercial and private vehicles to the army to help with the war effort. Their premises were then converted so that they could repair aircraft parts. They had around fifty people employed to specifically work on parts for Spitfires. They also had a mobile workshop so that they could visit any airfield in Cornwall that needed them for emergencies or repairs.

40. The Plaza

The cinema has always appealed to people, and Truro had several choices. Before 1900 the public rooms were the venue for Poole's Myriorama, who ran shows using light effects. In 1900, a travelling cinema came to town and in 1912 The Regal opened in the City Hall. In

The Plaza is a 1930s-style building in Georgian Lemon Street.

1921, the Palace cinema opened in the Palace Buildings, and it was in the early 1930s that the Plaza burst upon the citizens of Truro. The exterior of the building is art deco, a theme that continues inside. The luxury was something local folk had not experienced before. The elegant decor, uniformed staff, plush seats and carpets all gave the expectation of an excellent night out. By this time, gone were the little orchestra and pianist who made silent movies exciting; the 'talkies' had arrived and it was a new experience. These days there are more screens inside and a wider choice of films, making the super cinema that it was back then even more super.

At one time the large room above the cinema was a magnificent lighting shop with all manner of lampshades and chandeliers. In times past the entertainment in Lemon Street came from two public houses near Charles Street: the King's Head and the White Horse. With these now gone, just the Plaza and various restaurants remain to entertain the locals in this area.

There is always a choice of films or live streaming with several screens.

41. The Cricket Pavilion

Truro seems to have had a cricket club since 1810, but no one knows where they played their matches. We do know, however, that they had a pitch at Tremorvah for some years before 1900. Mr Chellew, the rather eccentric shipowner, let them play on his land until the beginning of the First World War, when cricket ceased until the end of hostilities. This was presumably because all the young men of an age to play the game had gone to war. When the game resumed after the war was over, Dick Chellew refused permission for them to play on his land again. There had been some sort of argument with the club and to ensure they could not play at Tremorvah again, he built a wall across the pitch. In view of this the cricket club made an agreement with Truro City Football Club, so until 1959 they played at Treyew Road where they had both a pitch and pavilion. It was during this period that W. G. Grace played at Truro for a special match. It was in 1959 that they leased the land still used by them today at Boscawen Park. It was leased from the city council and was part of the reclaimed land that meant the field was very uneven, and certainly not in a good enough state for a game of cricket. With much hard work from a dedicated band of volunteers, it became an excellent cricket ground with an excellent pitch and when the attractive pavilion was built in 1961 it became something Truro could be proud of. For many, Saturday afternoons were

The cricket pavilion in the sun waiting for the season to start.

The perfect choice of weathervane for the cricket club.

spent watching the game, although lots of the ladies also had a book or some knitting with them. The tea provided by the ladies was a sight to behold and enjoyed by all. The late Mr Christophers was a leading light during the transition from a reclaimed piece of land to a first-class cricket pitch. When he retired members clubbed together and bought him a car.

42. County Hall

Cornwall County Council was formed in 1888 and plans for a building to accommodate them were in hand not long after. In 1911, the building known as Old County Hall was built in Station Road. Most people remember it as a black building – no doubt it was covered in a layer of soot. It was soon outgrown and so the years 1925 and 1939 saw it being made bigger; however, it was still evidently not large enough as the grounds behind the building – leading up to Treyew Road – were soon peppered with an assortment of outbuildings. Today the Old County Hall has been sold and the soot has been washed away. Original plans were to turn it into a hotel, but that has not transpired yet. In 1965/6 the New County Hall arrived, set in attractive grounds, some of which had formerly been part of the gardens of Dalvenie House. This building has also sprouted some outbuildings in the grounds and a large car park. As the new premises are over fifty years old and it is now the only County Hall, with no need to differentiate between the two, dropping the word 'new' is preferred.

Above: Notices pointing to the entrance to County Hall.

Below: Saturday means an unusually empty car park at County Hall.

43. The Co-op

You may wonder what is so special about the Co-op supermarket in the middle of Boscawen Street. The answer is nothing really, but the style of the building is the ghost of what was once there. Until 1967, when a runaway lorry hurtled down Lemon Street, across Boscawen Street and straight into the front of the building, the stunning Red Lion – Truro's pride and joy – stood on the site. John Foote bought the land for it in 1682 and it was known as Mr Foote's Great House. In 1769, Edward Giddy put an announcement in the *Sherbourne Mercury*, the local newspaper, as he wanted his customers to know he was closing his hostelry, the Red Lion. The thirsty townsfolk were not inconvenienced, however, as Thomas Gatty opened up a new Red Lion two doors down the street in what had been Mr Foote's Great House. The Red Lion was the venue for many important occasions in Truro and many celebrations, birthdays, anniversaries, wedding receptions etc. took place there. It was also a favourite hotel with visitors and elegant motor cars – way out of financial reach for the local folk – often drawing up to the kerb. Supermarket trolleys are drawn up inside the door of the building now and shoppers wander up and down the aisles where once there was a magnificent staircase. There is a rear entrance to the shop too, so customers often leave that way as it is close to the car park.

Outside the Red Lion was always a good place to congregate and chat.

The Co-op in mock-Tudor style reminds us of what was once there.

44. Roman Catholic Church

This modern building dates from 1972. Years ago, the Roman Catholic Church building in Truro was small and unbefitting for the local worshippers, so Father Grainger bought a site with his own money. It was at the end of Dereham Terrace and the church is still there with the building that was the presbytery located next door. This church, recently used as a nursery, was in use for over seventy years but by 1972 the congregation had outgrown it and a new church was built in St Austell Street. The new building seats 340 people and has the dedication of Our Lady of the Portal and St Piran. Our Lady of the Portal is a rare dedication and is believed to come from Rome. It is thought that in medieval times a Truro merchant had a dangerous voyage to Rome and so, upon his safe arrival, he gave thanks and promised to build a church in Truro with the same dedication. For many years a chapel in what is now Old Bridge Street was known as Our Lady of the Portal, and alms given there helped to keep the old bridge in a good state of repair.

Our Lady and St Piran over the steps to the Roman Catholic Church.

Plenty of angles in the 1970s Roman Catholic Church.

45. Baptist Church, Chapel Hill

There have been Baptists in Truro since 1789 and in 1850 that they opened their new chapel, elegantly designed for them by the deaf and mute architect Philip Sambell. This chapel in River Street is now a café and is incorporated into the museum premises. In 1985, the congregation relocated to Chapel Hill on the site of what had been a pottery for many years. In fact, for quite some time the bottle kiln stood in the grounds of the Baptist Church. Dominican friars are believed to have started the pottery around 1250. Although nothing that old has been found on the site, an excavation in 1968 (to make a base for a new kiln) threw up some things of interest: the base of a kiln from 1670 was found, embedded into which was a 300-year-old piece of pot.

Around sixty years ago most schoolchildren knew that, if they were lucky, they would get a day out at the pottery where Mr Lake would be working and Mrs Lake would give the educational tour. Bernard Leach visited the pottery in the 1920s before he started his own in St Ives; he knew it was staffed by craftsmen who did things the old way and was interested in the way they worked, particularly by putting handles on pots. By the 1980s the traditional old pottery found it difficult to survive and even a museum on the premises did not last long. By this time it was known as Truro Pottery and was sold in 1984. The site

Above: A different style of architecture from the previous classical Baptist Church.

Below: The house of prayer next door to Bosvigo School.

was taken over by the Baptist Church, who seem proud of their heritage on the pottery land. It had been started by a religious order known as the Dominican friars, and became a place of worship that the friars would have understood.

46. Courts of Justice

Dominating the town is the court building, which was opened in 1988. It was once the site of the cattle market. In 1828, the town council wanted the market moved from High Cross. This did not find favour with the farmers, who were used to being close to the inns of the town – especially the Turks Head and the Unicorn, where they would call in for a few drinks as a market day treat. After one visit to Castle Hill they returned to High Cross, but by 1840 they had no choice and had to move. The new site on Castle Hill boasted a coffee shop, but this did not have the same appeal to the thirsty farmers. In 1983, work started to demolish the cattle market so that the building of the new court could begin. It is fitting that justice is dispensed today where it was meted out in the past. The castle built in the reign of King Stephen stood on this site and parts of its thick stone walls were cleared away in 1840 when the cattle market was being built. At that time it seemed that the fortification had probably been built on a much earlier Celtic structure.

Entrance to the court building that won an award in 1988.

47. Truro College

Truro College was opened in 1992 by Tim Boswell MP, Minister for Further and Higher Education. Being at Maiden Green, it was farther out of town than the two Truro schools that had closed to accommodate it. Truro County Grammar School for Girls had become the sixth form college of Richard Lander, but was demolished in 1993. Richard Lander School at Highertown was also knocked down and so gradually the college at Maiden Green got larger and larger. As well as having floodlit AstroTurf and a cricket academy, there are also other sporting opportunities, such as tennis and rugby. The buildings are all named after Cornish rivers. The main building is Mylor, which is the site of the main reception. Fal is the university building, and White is the art section, although every subject imaginable seems to be covered in the array of quirky buildings. The students of beauty and hairdressing are popular in town as they practise their skills on the local population.

The Lynher building at Truro College.

Named after the White River, the art building is unusual and attractive.

48. Truro Health Park

Truro Health Park was opened in September 2010 just above the old City Hospital on land that was given to the people of Truro for health purposes. For many years Truro had two surgeries in Lemon Street, known as top surgery and bottom surgery. They were both near the bottom end of Lemon Street and in easy reach of the town centre and although there was no dedicated parking, it was not needed as they were close to the town car parks and in many cases people walked to the doctor. The bottom surgery had two Cornish ranges in the waiting room, one fairly basic and the other equipped with brass knobs that gleamed against the black lead of the range. A Cornish range was an oven, hob and a fire all in one. They were often temperamental but could turn out a good meal or excellent bake depending on the skill of the housewife and the direction of the wind. As the surgeries became outdated and inadequate, work started on the new health park at the top of Infirmary Hill. There was much muttering and wondering how the patients were going to

Above: The side entrance to the surgeries has a chemist on site.

Below: A sit down might be needed after cycling up the hill!

A view of the leper's arch surrounded by new houses below the Health Park.

be able to struggle up either Infirmary Hill or Lemon Street, but with a car park attached to the building and a bus service, gradually people got used to it. The new building is large, with the doctors' surgeries to the left of the entrance and dentists to the right. All manner of health services are now under one roof: podiatry, physiotherapy and minor operations to name a few. There are lifts to make life easier for those who need them and attractive, coloured lights to gaze at while waiting for one's appointment. The surgeries are no longer referred to as top and bottom: top has become Lander Surgery and bottom is now Three Spires Surgery.

49. Waitrose

The coming of a Waitrose supermarket to Truro caused quite a stir. Although it is located just out of town because it is at the site of the Tregurra Park and Ride scheme, there is plenty of room to park the car close to the store. Many people remember the valley as a carpet of bluebells in the spring, but these are now all gone and under acres of tarmac. The valley was where Truro Water Co. had their pumping station and treatment works. An open leat fed water down the valley to large open settling filter beds. They were later filled in and grassed over. In the late 1880s Mr William John Lean worked for Truro Water Co. as their first formal engineer/manager, and his family lived in the house in the valley close to his work. A modern stone-built office on the site is now the ticket office for the park and ride scheme.

Above: This very smart supermarket has a section on the right for Cornish goods.

Below: The ticket office for Tregurra Park and Ride tickets.

50. Trevethow Riel

Truro has long been known as the finest Georgian city west of Bath and, during these times of widespread housebuilding, the reputation is still relevant. It is good that this group of new homes has been given a Cornish address (Trevethow Riel means 'royal crescent'). This crescent of new homes has been built overlooking Waitrose. Long before the building flurry of today, the valley was once home to people; however, the character of it has now changed and instead of homes in the valley, they are up above facing the Newquay Road. Behind the crescent are more new homes, built in the style of many old Truro cottages that have been cleared away during modernisation of the city.

New houses built in the style of many old Truro cottages.

Trevethow Riel is a crescent of new homes overlooking Tregurra Park and Ride.

Bibliography

Andrews, Dr C. T., *The First Cornish Hospital*.
Boscawen Street Area (Truro Buildings Research Group).
From Moresk Road to Malpas (Truro Buildings Research Group).
Lemon Street and its Neighbourhood (Truro Buildings Research Group).
Parnell, Christine, *History and Guide Truro*.
Princes Street and the Quay Area (Truro Buildings Research Group).
Pydar Street and the High Cross Area (Truro Buildings Research Group).
River Street and its Neighbourhood (Truro Buildings Research Group).

About the Author

Christine Parnell has been interested in the history of Cornwall – especially Truro – since her inclusion in a team of girls from Truro County Grammar School to represent Truro in a Westward Television local knowledge quiz programme. She enjoyed learning about her area and in the following two years represented Truro on two more quiz programmes, one for the BBC and one for ITV. She joined the Truro Old Cornwall Society at the age of fourteen and although her late husband's work took her away from Truro for some years, she has now been the secretary of the society for twenty-three years. This is her tenth book about Truro and she has also co-authored one with Diana Smith about Veryan and Portloe.